CHARLIE BROWN'S 'CYCLOPEDIA

Super Questions and Answers and Amazing Facts

Featuring
Space Travel

Volume 7

Based on the Charles M. Schulz Characters

Funk & Wagnalls, Inc.

Photograph and Illustration Credits: Lockheed Missiles and Space Company, 332; National Aeronautics and Space Administration, 291, 295, 298, 303, 304, 305, 306, 307, 313, 316, 317, 323, 324, 327, 336, xi; Tass from Sovfoto, 315.

A large part of the material in this volume was previously published in *Charlie Brown's Second Super Book of Questions and Answers.*

Introduction

Welcome to volume 7 of *Charlie Brown's 'Cyclopedia*! Have you ever wondered what a space shuttle is, or what LEM means, or what astronauts eat? Charlie Brown and the rest of the *Peanuts* gang are here to help you find the answers to these questions and many more about space travel. Have fun!

What is meant by the "space age"?

The space age began when rocket ships were first sent out into space. In 1957, Russia sent Sputnik I into space to circle the earth. After that, a dog named Laika and a monkey named Sam became the first living space travelers.

The first person to fly around the earth in outer space was a Russian named Yuri Gagarin (gah-GAH-rin), in 1961. A month later, Alan B. Shepard became the first American to go into outer space. Since then, many other people have traveled in space. So we say that we are living in the space age.

What is space?

To most people the word "space" means the huge emptiness that is all around the earth. But space is not only out among the faraway stars. It is also right close to home. Whenever you go from one place to another, you are moving through space.

Is there an end to space?

Scientists don't know for sure. The part of space that begins about 100 miles (160 kilometers) above the earth is usually called outer space. The part of outer space among the planets is called interplanetary (in-tur-PLAN-ih-ter-ee) space. It spreads out for about 4,000,000,000 (4 billion) miles (more than 6 billion kilometers). It includes the nine planets that travel around our sun. Even farther out is deep space. That is where the stars are.

How far out does space go? There's no way to tell.

Who owns outer space?

We all do! Most of the powerful countries of the world have agreed that outer space should belong to everybody.

Why do people explore space?

People have always been curious about unknown places. At one time, people living in one place on earth knew very little about the rest of the world. But they wanted to learn as much as they could. So sailors traveled the seas and discovered new lands. Explorers journeyed through the western part of the United States and to the North and South poles. Now we can say that almost every part of our world is known.

Today there are new worlds to discover. People want to know what is out in space. They want to find out more about the planets and the stars.

Spacecraft have already landed on Venus and Mars. Even though no astronauts were on board, these spacecraft sent back scientific information and pictures. Astronauts have walked on the moon. In the future, people will be able to travel to the planets, hoping to find out still more about unknown places.

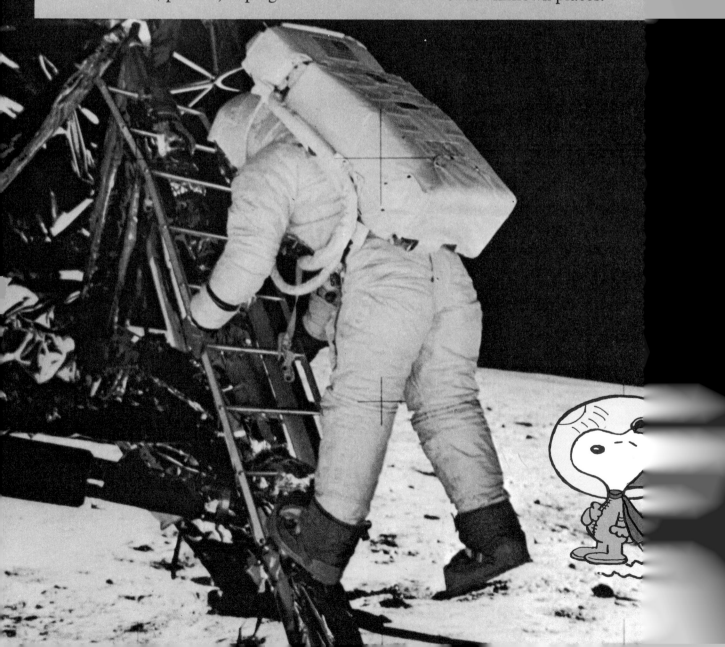

Can an airplane fly in outer space?

No. An airplane is held up by air that streams around the wings as the plane moves forward. Above the ground, the air starts to thin out. At 20 or 30 miles (32 or 48 kilometers) up, the air becomes too thin to hold up an airplane. Beyond 100 miles (160 kilometers), there is almost no air at all. So an airplane cannot fly there.

What does the sky look like in outer space?

If you were in outer space, you would see the sun, the moon, and the stars bright in a black sky—all the time. On earth, the daytime sky does not look black. The air scatters sunlight all around, which brightens up the sky and makes it seem blue. The sky around other planets may appear to be other colors. Different gases hang over each planet and scatter the sunlight in different ways. But far from a planet, there are no gases, so there can be no scattering of light. The sky looks black.

Pictures of the planet Mars show that its sky is orange-pink!

SIGH

Is outer space hot or cold?

Everything whirling in space is hot or cold or in between. Stars are like huge furnaces. When heat streams out from them and reaches anything in space, that thing gets hot, too. That's why planets close to a star are hot or warm. The farther a planet is from a star, the colder that planet is. Most of outer space is not heated by stars. It is very cold—nearly 460 degrees below zero Fahrenheit ($-460°$ F., or $-275°$ C.).

Are there sounds in outer space?

No. When something vibrates—shakes back and forth quickly—in the air, movements called sound waves are sent out. The sound waves move through the air to your ears. Then you hear the sound. But outer space has no air to carry sound waves. So you cannot hear any sounds.

! Huge explosions are always taking place on the sun.
If there were air all the way from the sun to the earth,
we would hear the roar of these explosions all the time! !

Are there clouds in space?

There are clouds, but not like the ones near the earth. Warm, moist air floats upward from the earth and cools off. Some of that moisture then gathers into small water drops or bits of ice. Many of these drops of water and bits of ice together form a cloud. Most clouds are only a few miles above the ground.

In outer space there is no water, so clouds of moisture do not form. But there are huge clouds of gas and dust in deep space. They hide some of the distant stars from us.

The earth with clouds, as seen from space

What is radiation?

Scientists use the word radiation (ray-dee-AY-shun) for anything that flows outward—much like the spray of water from a garden hose. All radiation travels in the form of waves. An example of this is light, streaming from the sun or from a lamp. Another example is the heat that comes out of the sun. Radio and television broadcasts move through wires and through the air as streams of radiation.

Is there radiation in outer space?

Yes, outer space is crisscrossed by many kinds of radiation. There are light waves. There are x-rays—just like the ones the doctor uses to take pictures of your insides. And there are other kinds of radiation, too—all moving through space at about 11 million miles (almost 18 million kilometers) a minute.

Is radiation dangerous?

In outer space, most kinds of radiation are very dangerous. People cannot live if the radiation hits them directly. Astronauts must be protected by their spacecraft or spacesuit at all times. Here on earth, the air protects us from nearly all the harmful rays. Even so, some of them can get through and cause bad sunburn.

What are radiation belts?

All around the earth there are two invisible clouds made up of very tiny specks called electrons and protons. These specks are so small that you cannot see them, even under a microscope! The clouds they make up are called radiation belts.

Inside the belts, the radiation is deadly. It is thousands of times stronger than a person could stand. Astronauts are protected by their spacecraft if they must pass through the belts on their way to outer space. Usually they can steer their spacecraft away from the belts through escape zones.

There are very large, strong radiation belts around the planet Jupiter. Other planets may have them, too.

297

What other dangers are there in space?

There are bits of rock, called meteoroids (MEE-tee-uh-roidz), flying around everywhere in outer space. Many of them are no bigger than a grain of sand. Some move hundreds of times as fast as a rifle bullet. They go so fast that even the smallest ones can do great damage to anything they hit.

What is a spaceport?

A port is a place where ships stay before a trip. Ships also load at a port and leave from a port. So a "spaceport" is a place where "spaceships" stay before a trip, where they load, and from which they take off. A spaceport has hangars —buildings where spacecraft are kept. It also has storage tanks for rocket fuel and room for all the other equipment needed for space travel. The main American spaceport is at Cape Canaveral (kuh-NAV-er-ull), Florida.

Kennedy Space Center, Cape Canaveral

298

What is the difference between a spacecraft and a spaceship?

The two words mean the same thing—any rocket-powered machine that can carry people or material in space. The word "spacecraft" is usually used in talking about a real rocket-powered machine. For example, astronauts went to the moon in an Apollo spacecraft. The word "spaceship" is used mainly in science-fiction stories.

What does a spacecraft look like?

These are pictures of a few different kinds of spacecraft with the rockets that sent them into space. You can see how large they were by comparing them with the size of the man. The Apollo 5 with its rocket was 363 feet (111 meters) tall—as high as a 45-story building. It weighed more than 3,000 tons (2,700 metric tons).

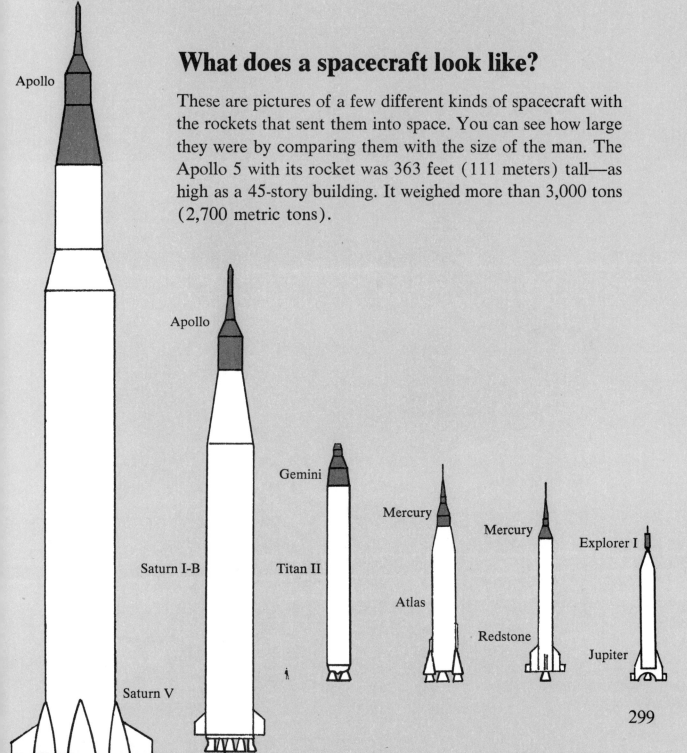

Apollo

Saturn V

Apollo

Saturn I-B

Gemini

Titan II

Mercury

Atlas

Mercury

Redstone

Explorer I

Jupiter

299

What is a rocket?

A rocket is a kind of engine, or motor, that is powerful enough to lift a very heavy spacecraft off the earth. In order to do this, it burns special fuels, just as an automobile burns gasoline as fuel. But a rocket may need up to ten million times more fuel than an automobile does!

Sometimes the word "rocket" is used to mean any rocket engine. Sometimes "rocket" is used to mean the main rocket engines of a spacecraft. And at other times people use the word to mean the rocket engines along with the rest of the spacecraft.

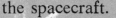

Fireworks rocket

Goddard rocket

Who made the first rocket?

Nobody knows exactly. The Chinese were using rockets more than 800 years ago. These rockets were powered by gunpowder. They were like the skyrockets that you see in Fourth of July fireworks shows.

In 1903, a Russian schoolteacher named K. E. Tsiolkovsky (tzawl-KAWF-skee) had the idea of using rockets for flights into space. In 1926, the American scientist Robert H. Goddard sent up a rocket that went about as high as a 20-story building.

WOW! LOOK AT THOSE ROCKETS!

FANTASTIC!

HAPPINESS IS THE FIREWORKS DISPLAY O THE FOURTH OF JULY

How does a rocket work?

Strangely, in order for something to move in one direction, it must give a push in the opposite direction. When you row a boat, you push the water in the opposite direction from the way you want to go. When you swim in a pool, you sometimes push back against the pool wall to move you forward quickly.

This kind of two-way action is what makes a rocket motor work. Fuel is burned inside the rocket. This is called "firing" the rocket. The burning fuel forms great clouds of hot gas. The heat makes the gases swell up. They need more room, and they can escape only through an opening at the back of the rocket. So, as the gases rush out at the back, the spacecraft is pushed forward.

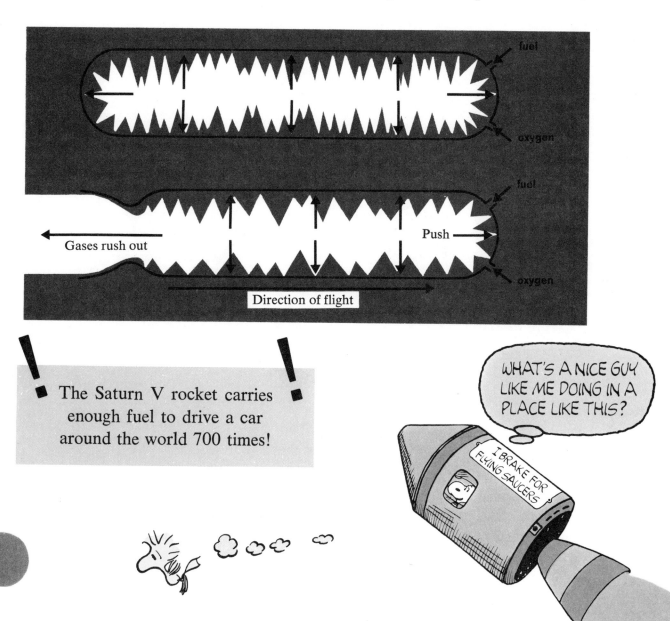

fuel

oxygen

fuel

Gases rush out

Push

oxygen

Direction of flight

The Saturn V rocket carries enough fuel to drive a car around the world 700 times!

WHAT'S A NICE GUY LIKE ME DOING IN A PLACE LIKE THIS?

I BRAKE FOR FLYING SAUCERS

301

What is a countdown?

A countdown is a check-up time before a spacecraft is sent up from the earth. During this time, every inch of the rocket and spaceship is tested to see that it is in perfect working order. All the machinery that sets off and guides the ship is tested, too. A green light is switched on for each part that is in good working order. If something is not working properly, the countdown stops until that part is fixed. A person speaking over a loudspeaker keeps telling everyone at the spaceport how many hours and minutes of countdown are left.

A countdown may take hours or even days. It will continue until all the dials flash a green light. Finally the loudspeaker booms, "10—9—8—7—6—5—4—3—2—1—ZERO!" This instant is called T-zero (Time-zero). With a loud roar the rocket blasts off and the ship begins to rise.

What is an orbit?

The path of one object in space around another is called an orbit. The planets move in orbits around the sun. Each planet's orbit is shaped something like an egg.

The earth takes a year to go once around its orbit. Planets closer to the sun take less time than this. Planets farther away take longer.

Now, in the space age, we can send spacecraft into orbit around the earth, the moon, and the planets.

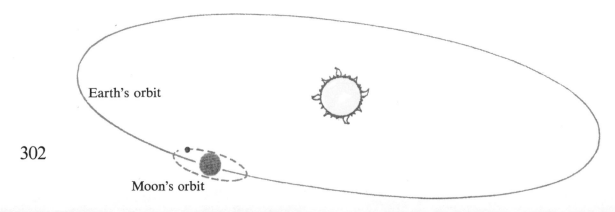

Earth's orbit

Moon's orbit

How is a spacecraft sent into orbit?

This is done in three steps. Each step is called a stage. Here's how an Apollo spacecraft would be sent into orbit around the earth before going on to the moon.

First-stage rockets are sometimes called boosters. They give the spacecraft a powerful push that lifts it from the ground. In two and a half minutes, the spacecraft is 40 miles (64 kilometers) up. It is then going 6,000 miles (9,600 kilometers) an hour. At that time the first-stage rockets stop firing. They are dropped off into the ocean. This makes the spacecraft lighter and saves power on the rest of the trip.

Next, the second-stage rockets fire for six minutes. Then they are dropped off, too. The spacecraft is now about 110 miles (176 kilometers) up, going over 14,000 miles (22,400 kilometers) an hour.

The third-stage rockets are then fired for about two minutes. This gets the spacecraft to a height of 120 miles (192 kilometers) and a speed of about 17,500 miles (28,000 kilometers) an hour. It is now in orbit around the earth, going about 30 times as fast as a jet plane.

The third-stage rockets stay in place on the spacecraft. Later, they will take it to the moon and back. These rockets are attached to the part of the spacecraft called the modules (MOJ-oolz)—the command module, the service module, and the lunar module.

Apollo 15 lift-off

The first-stage Apollo rocket motor is as powerful as 640,000 car engines!

What is a command module?

A command module is the front end of a spacecraft where the astronauts live and do their work. This module is like the cockpit of an airplane and is sometimes called a space capsule. The command module of a spacecraft that goes to the moon has more than two million working parts. An automobile has fewer than two thousand.

What is a service module?

A service module is the part of a spacecraft that carries batteries for electric power. This power is needed for air conditioning, heating, and lighting. The service module also has tanks of oxygen for the astronauts to breathe.

What is a lunar module?

A lunar module is the part of the spacecraft that actually lands astronauts on the moon. It is usually called the LEM, and it is carried inside the third stage of the spacecraft.

After the spacecraft goes into orbit around the moon, the LEM separates from the spacecraft and starts a downward trip. Not all the astronauts go along. One must stay behind to run the orbiting spacecraft.

When the LEM reaches the landing place, its rockets are fired to let it settle down gently on the moon.

The LEM on the moon

Just before it touches down, the LEM is moving more slowly than a falling leaf!

I THOUGHT HE'D NEVER GET OUT OF THE ORBIT.

What happens to the parts of a spacecraft that are dropped off?

As a spacecraft goes up, man-made objects such as rocket stages are left behind in space. The first ones dropped are slowed down by the air. Some of these burn up as they fall. Others splash down into the ocean.

The pieces that are let loose high up go into orbit around the earth. These are known as space junk. They may last for a year or longer before they drop down and burn up. There are more than 3,000 pieces of space junk still in orbit.

A space walk

MIKE COLLINS LITTERS!

During a space walk in 1969, astronaut Michael Collins happened to let go of his camera. It became an expensive piece of space junk!

How is a spacecraft steered?

This is usually done by turning the main rocket motors that are at the bottom of the spacecraft. To turn the spacecraft just a little, special small rockets on the sides are fired. All of these steering rockets can be worked by the astronauts or by radio signals from the ground.

HERE'S THE WORLD-FAMOUS ASTRONAUT TAKING OFF FOR THE MOON...

ALL SYSTEMS ARE GO! A-OK! HOW DO YOU READ? LOUD AND CLEAR!

WE HAVE LIFT OFF! THE BIRD IS BEGINNING TO MOVE....

WE HAVE A LOT OF "IN" EXPRESSIONS!

What is "mission control"?

All space flights are run from a center called mission control. The people in charge of the flight work at this center.

Mission control does not have to be at the spaceport. It can be hundreds of miles away. The people at mission control talk with the astronauts by two-way radio. This means that the astronauts and the people at mission control have radios that do two things—send out messages and pick up messages. The mission control people watch signal lights and special TV screens to keep track of the flight.

What is NASA?

NASA stands for the National Aeronautics (air-uh-NAW-ticks) and Space Administration. This organization is the part of the United States government that is in charge of exploring space. Thousands of scientists and engineers work for NASA.

How does NASA keep track of a traveling spacecraft?

Radio signals from the spacecraft are picked up by stations on earth. These stations are at several places around the world. Some of the receivers are on ships at sea.

The signals are sent into a computer. It figures out where the spacecraft is at any time.

Can spacecraft be sent to the planets?

Yes. In 1976, an American spacecraft called the Viking landed on the planet Mars. Another spacecraft, Pioneer-Saturn, is now on the way to Saturn and should arrive there in 1979. It has already flown past Jupiter and sent back scientific information. Later, the United States will send another Pioneer to Venus to find out more about this planet. The Russians have already sent two spacecraft, Venera 3 and Venera 4, to Venus. But both crash-landed.

Spacecraft do not have to land on a planet to be useful. They can carry telescopes that take pictures as they pass close to a planet. These pictures are very clear and much better than any taken by telescopes on earth.

Will people ever be able to visit other planets?

Yes, but it will not be easy. A trip will take many months—even to one of the nearest planets, Venus or Mars. The chances are better for a visit to Mars than for a visit to Venus. Although Mars is much colder than the earth, a spacesuit can probably keep people warm enough. But Venus is hotter than the inside of a furnace. A spacesuit would not help there!

What is gravity?

Gravity is a force that every planet, star, and moon has. This force causes everything on or near the planet, star, or moon to be pulled downward.

The pull of the earth's gravity holds the moon in its orbit. The pull of the sun's gravity keeps the planets in their orbits.

Stand on a bathroom scale. Suppose it shows that you weigh 90 pounds (41 kilograms). This means that the downward pull of the earth's gravity on your body measures 90 pounds (41 kilograms).

What is a satellite?

Anything in space that moves in an orbit is called a satellite (SAT-uh-lite). The earth is a satellite of the sun. So are the other planets in our solar system because they orbit the sun. The moon is a satellite of the earth because it orbits the earth. Seven of the planets have satellites moving around them. The earth has only one moon, but Saturn has ten. Jupiter has thirteen! And more moons may be discovered. All these are called natural satellites.

There are also artificial (ahr-tuh-FISH-ull) satellites. The word "artificial" means man-made. Artificial satellites are built on earth and put into orbit. Since the beginning of the space age, hundreds of artificial satellites have been sent into space—weather satellites, TV satellites, and many other kinds.

(satellite of Earth)
Moon

Sun

Earth
(satellite of the Sun)

Natural satellites

Artificial satellite

311

What was the first satellite to orbit the earth?

The moon, of course! It is the earth's natural satellite and has been in orbit for billions of years. The first artificial earth satellite, called Sputnik I, was sent up by Russia in 1957. A few months later, the first American satellite, Explorer I, was sent into orbit. After a while, both of these satellites slowed up and dropped closer to the earth. As they fell through the air, they became so hot that they burned up.

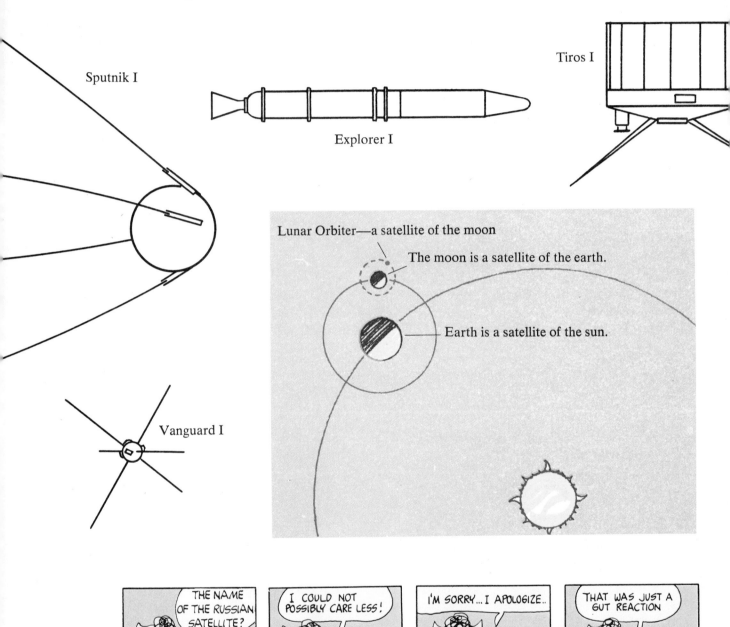

Sputnik I

Explorer I

Tiros I

Lunar Orbiter—a satellite of the moon

The moon is a satellite of the earth.

Earth is a satellite of the sun.

Vanguard I

THE NAME OF THE RUSSIAN SATELLITE?

I COULD NOT POSSIBLY CARE LESS!

I'M SORRY... I APOLOGIZE..

THAT WAS JUST A GUT REACTION

What do artificial satellites do?

Weather satellites orbit the earth several hundred miles up. They measure the temperature and amount of moisture, or dampness, in the air. They send back TV pictures showing where there are clouds and storms on earth.

Communications satellites pick up electrical waves from TV stations. The waves bounce back to distant places on earth. That is how you get "live" TV broadcasts from halfway around the world. Some communications satellites are used for sending long-distance telephone calls.

Some scientific satellites measure radiations from outer space that do not get through the air to the ground. Other scientific satellites carry telescopes that send back pictures of planets and stars. These pictures are much clearer than any taken from earth.

A scientific satellite

313

What is a cosmonaut?

A cosmonaut is a Russian space traveler. The word comes from two Greek words that mean "sailor of the universe." An American space traveler is called an astronaut. The word means "sailor among the stars."

How can you become an astronaut?

If you want to become an astronaut, you must be less than 34 years old, intelligent, and in perfect health. You must have a good education and go through a long testing and training period.

Astronauts must study science and engineering and have at least 1,000 hours of experience flying jet airplanes.

The special training that astronauts get is very difficult. Many are forced to drop out before finishing.

Has a woman ever traveled in space?

Yes. A woman named Valentina Tereshkova (tay-RESH-koe-vah) was one of the cosmonauts in the Russian spacecraft Vostok 6 that orbited the earth in 1963.

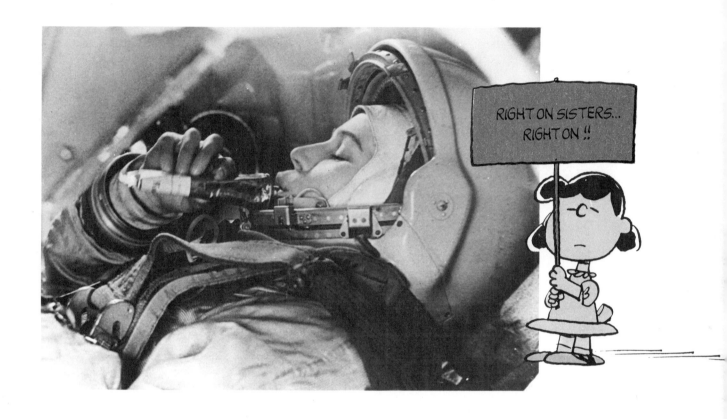

Will there be other women in space?

Probably. In the 1980s, the United States plans to send people into space and back fairly often. NASA is already training a group of air force nurses. They will live and work for a while in space stations that will orbit the earth. These stations will be places for space research. They will also serve as hotels for travelers going from one part of space to another.

Why do astronauts wear spacesuits?

The main purpose of spacesuits is to keep astronauts healthy and comfortable when they are not inside the spacecraft. Each suit is airtight. It keeps the air, the temperature, and the pressure inside the suit as earthlike as possible. The astronauts also wear helmets that have a gold coating on the front. This protects them from the rays of the sun.

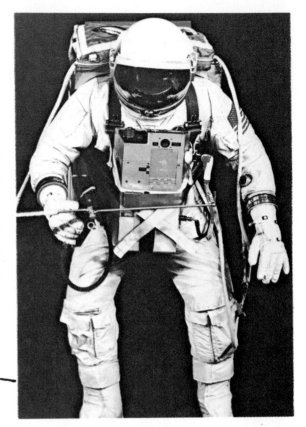

Can astronauts take off their spacesuits during a trip?

Yes, if the astronauts stay inside the spacecraft. Of course, they must be "suited up" again when they get ready to take a space walk or land on the moon. They help each other put on the bulky suit. If they are going far from the spaceship, they also hook up a backpack. The pack holds air for breathing, heating and cooling equipment, and radio equipment for contact with earth and with other astronauts.

What is a space walk?

When astronauts go outside their orbiting spacecraft, we say they are taking a space walk. Of course, they are not really walking at all. They are only drifting alongside the spacecraft. Each drifting astronaut is connected to the spacecraft by a long hose. The hose keeps the astronaut from floating off into space. It also takes the place of a backpack. The hose has electric lines for air conditioning and radio. It also has an air tube for breathing. To get back to the spacecraft, the astronauts slowly pull themselves along their hose.

What is a life-support system?

A life-support system has everything that astronauts need in order to stay alive in space. It is the part of a spacecraft that keeps conditions very much as they are on earth.

A life-support system has water, air, and food for the astronauts. It keeps the temperature comfortable. It also protects the astronauts from harmful radiations in space.

The astronauts' backpacks are smaller life-support systems. Astronauts use these outside the spacecraft.

Why do things float around in a spacecraft?

On earth, gravity holds everything down. While a spacecraft is orbiting, the earth's gravity is still pulling on everything in the craft. But another force, which comes from orbiting, also pulls on everything. The two forces are equal and cause everything—and everyone—to float. This kind of floating is called weightlessness. All things inside a spacecraft float around if they are not held down.

FLOATING AROUND IN SPACE CAN BE VERY EXCITING... AFTER A FEW YEARS, HOWEVER, THE EXCITEMENT WEARS OFF!

What do astronauts eat?

Freeze-dried foods are used to save space and to keep things fresh. The food is first frozen, and the ice that forms is then taken out. The astronauts just add water to freeze-dried food, and it is ready to eat.

In an orbiting spacecraft, eating is tricky because of weightlessness. Astronauts cannot drink from an open cup. The liquid forms blobs that float around and wet anything they hit. So drinks must be kept in closed plastic bags. Astronauts must squeeze the liquid right into their mouth. Solid foods are in bite-sized pieces so that crumbs will not float around and pollute the air in the spacecraft.

For long trips, astronauts may someday grow their own food plants in the spacecraft.

How do astronauts get rid of body wastes?

Liquid waste is pumped into space, where it becomes a gas. Solid waste is put into plastic bags with chemicals that kill germs. The bags are thrown away when the spacecraft returns to earth.

How are astronauts made ready for space travel?

Scientists have set up labs on earth that copy the way astronauts will live when they are in space. For example, an astronaut is put inside a large metal ball. The ball is spun in order to put a great push on the astronaut's body. It is like the push people feel when a spacecraft zooms upward. Astronauts also move around under water in spacesuits. That helps them get used to the feel of floating weightless in space.

Also, astronauts work in an exact copy of a command module. They practice using the dials and switches that will control the spacecraft.

The dashboard of a car has only about half a dozen switches and signal lights on it. The instrument panel of the Apollo command module has more than 600!

What is space medicine?

This is the science that takes care of the health of astronauts. Much can be found out in advance about how space will affect the health of space travelers. Doctors study the people being trained in labs on earth. Doctors also check the health of astronauts when they are in space and when they return to earth.

How do doctors check astronauts in space?

Electrical machines connected to the body of an astronaut check his breathing, heartbeat, and temperature. Readings are automatically sent back by radio to doctors on earth.

What does space travel do to an astronaut's thoughts and feelings?

When an astronaut is alone in space for many, many days, he may become very upset. He might even panic. Sometimes things look blurry to him. He feels strange, and things around him do not seem real.

Even if an astronaut is not alone, he may get very tense and grouchy. For this reason, the people who will someday work in satellites called space stations will have to be sent back to earth after about a month. Other astronauts will be sent up to take their places.

Why is an astronaut sometimes strapped to his couch?

This is done only during lift-off and return to earth. At those times the astronaut's body feels a great push. It is the same kind of push that you feel when you ride in a car that makes a sudden, fast start. It seems as if you are being shoved back into your seat.

The pushing forces are much, much stronger in a spacecraft that is leaving or coming back to earth. The astronaut feels a force of nearly a ton on his body! That is why he must be supported by a couch during take-off and landing.

How long can people stay in space?

Scientists do not yet know for sure. In 1973, a spacecraft named the Skylab was sent into orbit around the earth. There were four men in it. They lived and worked there for almost a month and were in good health when they returned to earth. Other astronaut teams have spent nearly three months in orbit.

There will be many more problems in sending astronauts farther out into space. A trip to a planet will take many months, or even years.

A trip to the nearest star would take a whole lifetime, even if the spacecraft could travel 100,000 miles (160,000 kilometers) a second!

What does the "docking" of two spacecraft mean?

Two spacecraft in orbit can meet and link together. They use their small rocket motors to line up. Then they slowly move toward each other until they can lock together. This is called docking.

In 1975, an American Apollo docked with a Russian Soyuz (SOY-use) in orbit 138 miles (221 kilometers) above the earth. Then the astronauts and the cosmonauts visited back and forth between the two spacecraft.

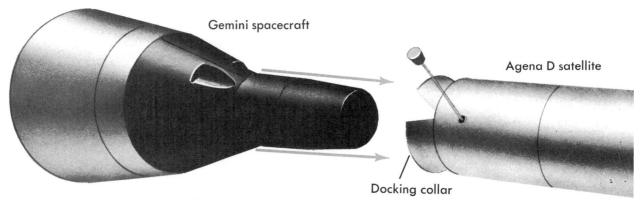

Gemini spacecraft

Agena D satellite

Docking collar

How long does a spacecraft take to go to the moon and back?

The first manned flight to the moon took about four days from the time the spacecraft left the earth until it went into orbit around the moon. The return trip took a little less than three days.

Who was the first person to step onto the moon?

The first person to step onto the moon was Astronaut Neil Armstrong, when he climbed down from the Apollo 11 landing craft on July 20, 1969. Since that time, ten men have walked on the moon.

Neil Armstrong

What does the moon look like close up?

The moon is very rough and rocky. There are tall mountains, deep cracks, and steep cliffs. All over the moon are thousands of scooped-out holes shaped like saucers. These holes are called craters. Many of them were formed when rocks, flying through space, crashed onto the moon. Most of these rocks exploded when they hit the moon. Bits of them were scattered all over. So you cannot find the rocks, but you can see the holes they made. Some craters are less than a foot (30 centimeters) wide. The biggest ones are more than 150 miles (240 kilometers) wide.

There are some large, smooth places on the moon called "seas." These have no water in them, just rocks and soil. The seas were formed by melted rock that spread out, cooled, and became hard. The melted rock may have come up from the hot inside part of the moon. Or large rocks that crashed onto the moon may have melted from the heat of the crash.

Moon rover

Two million football stadiums could fit inside the largest moon crater!

How do astronauts talk to each other on the moon?

They use the small radio that is built into each spacesuit. Radios work on the moon because radio waves can travel even where there is no air.

As astronauts talk to each other, mission control listens in. The people on earth answer questions and tell the astronauts what to do.

Could an astronaut hitchhike on the moon?

Yes, if another astronaut happened to be coming along in a moon rover. The rover looks like a jeep or a dune buggy. It gets its power from batteries. On one moon expedition, astronauts David Scott and James Irwin traveled more than 17 miles (27 kilometers) in their moon rover. They collected moon rocks to take back to earth.

Is there gravity on the moon?

Yes. But the moon is much smaller than the earth, so its gravity is much weaker. If you weighed 90 pounds (41 kilograms) here on earth, you would weigh only about 15 pounds (7 kilograms) on the moon.

Why do astronauts shuffle along instead of walk on the moon?

Because the moon's gravity does not pull as strongly as the earth's gravity, astronauts cannot walk on the moon the same way they walk on earth. If they did, they would rise a few feet off the ground with every step. They can keep better control and stay on the ground by just shuffling along. If astronauts did not have to wear their heavy spacesuit and backpack, they could jump 35 feet (11 meters) high.

Apollo-Saturn 1 at Cape Canaveral

Gemini VII spacecraft

David R. Scott and Apollo 9

Astronaut Edwin Aldrin on the moon

Athletes on the moon
could leap over a two-story house.
And they would come down no harder
than they had after a 6-foot
(180-centimeter) jump on earth!

WOW, EVEN A LITTLE GUY LIKE ME COULD BREAK ALL HIGH JUMPING RECORDS... ON THE MOON, THAT IS.

How do astronauts leave the moon?

When astronauts finish their moon work, they blast off in the LEM. It goes up to meet the main spacecraft that is orbiting the moon. The two ships dock together and the astronauts board the command module. The LEM is left behind as space junk. The third-stage rockets on the service module are then fired, and the spacecraft heads back toward earth.

How a spacecraft gets out of orbit.

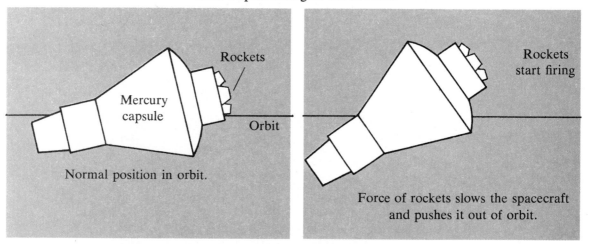

Rockets

Mercury capsule

Orbit

Normal position in orbit.

Rockets start firing

Force of rockets slows the spacecraft and pushes it out of orbit.

What is re-entry?

As a spacecraft returns from outer space, it must plunge into the air before it can land. This is called re-entry.

What is the heat shield on a spacecraft?

When a returning spacecraft plunges back into the earth's air, its gets extremely hot. To protect the astronauts, the front end of the capsule is covered with a heat shield made of special plastic. The shield heats up to about 5,000 degrees Fahrenheit (5,000° F., or 2,700° C.). Some of the plastic melts and burns off, taking away the dangerous heat. Inside the capsule, the temperature stays at a comfortable 80 degrees Fahrenheit (27° C.).

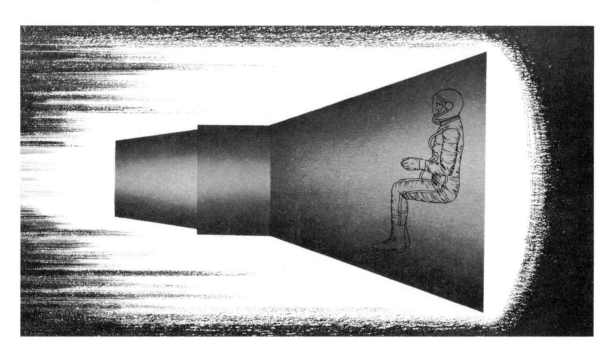

Can the astronauts talk with mission control during landing?

Astronauts and mission control talk back and forth by radio right up to the time the spacecraft comes back into the air. Then, as the heat shield begins to get hot, a strange thing happens. A cloud of tiny electrical bits gathers around the command module. Radio waves cannot get through this cloud. So, for several minutes, there is only silence between the astronauts and the ground.

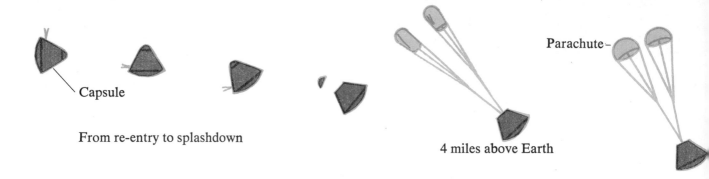

Capsule

From re-entry to splashdown

4 miles above Earth

Parachute

How does a returning spacecraft make a safe landing?

As the spacecraft gets ready to enter the air again, the service module is thrown off and left in space. Now all that is left is the command module—the capsule —with the astronauts in it.

Before re-entry, the capsule is turned around so that the end with the heat shield faces forward. This is done by firing small steering rockets. As the capsule enters the air, it does not point straight toward the ground, it comes in on a slanting path.

Now a computer takes over the steering. If the capsule were aimed too low, it might fall downward, get too hot, and burn up. If it were aimed too high, it might bounce off the upper layers of the air and be thrown back into space. Because it no longer has its powerful main rocket motor, the capsule would not have the force behind it to return to earth.

At the time of re-entry, the capsule is moving at 25,000 miles (40,000 kilometers) an hour. For a safe landing, this enormous speed must be cut down to only a few miles an hour. Rubbing against the air makes the capsule lose most of its speed. Then, about 4 miles (6 kilometers) above the earth, two small parachutes open. They slow the falling motion even more. They also keep the capsule from wobbling. About 2 miles (3 kilometers) up, three big parachutes open. The capsule floats down to earth at a safe speed.

What is "splashdown"?

This is the moment a capsule lands in the earth's water. As soon as splashdown takes place, ships and helicopters rush to the floating capsule. Divers jump into the water and place a doughnut-shaped balloon around the capsule to make sure it does not sink. The astronauts open a door called a hatch, and are lifted into a helicopter. They are taken to a nearby ship. Their space trip is over.

Up to now, all American spacecraft landings have been made on the ocean. The Russian cosmonauts bring their spacecraft down on land.

The Apollo capsule was tested for splashdown by dropping it into a tank of water from a tower 18 stories high!

2 miles above Earth

331

What is a space station?

It is a special kind of satellite that will circle the earth a few hundred miles up. One kind of space station will be shaped like a huge ring, hundreds of feet across. It will be put together in orbit after the parts are sent up from the ground.

The station will be turning as it moves along its orbit around the earth. The turning motion will create a kind of gravity. It will allow people to walk around as on earth, instead of being weightless and floating.

What will a space station be used for?

A space station will be a place where scientists can work in space. It will also be a stopping-off place for spacecraft that are going farther out into space. The inside of the space station will be divided into science workrooms and labs. There will also be dormitories, kitchens, and even a gym.

Will there be factories in space?

Probably. They will be useful in making things that are hard to make on earth. For example, metals can be joined together by heating them. This is called welding. If a weld is to be strong, the pieces must not be touched by air during the joining. On earth, small objects can be welded in a closed box with the air pumped out. Many things are too big to be welded this way. But welding would be easy in a factory where there is no air—on the moon or on a space station orbiting the earth.

What is a space shuttle?

A space shuttle is a spacecraft that will travel back and forth between the ground and an orbiting space station. It will carry people and heavy loads of material. It will have wings and be about as big as a jet plane.

As a shuttle heads upward, some of its rockets will drop back to earth by parachute. These rockets will be used again and again.

When starting its return trip, the shuttle will fire a rocket motor and zoom safely through the air, protected by a heat shield. Then the shuttle will land on a runway, as an ordinary airplane does.

An airplane trip in the United States costs about 20 cents a mile (12 cents a kilometer). A trip on the shuttle may cost 10 dollars a mile (6 dollars a kilometer). If so, a trip to the moon and back would cost more than 4 million dollars!

OF COURSE, YOU COULD SAVE TWO MILLION WITH A ONE WAY TICKET!

What is a space colony?

A space colony is a kind of island in space where thousands of people can live and work. No space colony exists yet, but the United States and Russia are both planning colonies.

Each space colony will be a huge aluminum tube half a mile (nearly a kilometer) long, orbiting the earth. The tube will keep turning slowly to give the feeling of gravity. Large mirrors will focus the sun's rays and provide all the power for electricity needed by the colony. Once the colony is set up, people will not need to bring many new things from the earth. They will raise their own food crops and farm animals. They will be able to get minerals and other building materials from mines on the moon. So people in space colonies will be helping the earth save food, minerals, and other natural resources.

Why should we build space colonies?

In a space colony, there will be plenty of food. There will be no earthquakes, no floods, and no storms. So a space colony will be a safer place to live than earth is.

A space colony will have sunlight 24 hours a day. The sun's rays will give the colony all the power it needs to run its machines. If the world ever becomes too crowded, people can move to space colonies.

 You and your family could be living in a space colony by the time you reach middle age!

Are there people living somewhere else in space?

Scientists do not know of any place in the universe besides the earth where there is life. But hundreds of billions of stars are in the universe. Millions of these stars may have planets orbiting around them. It is very likely that on many of those planets conditions are right for some kind of life.

There could be intelligent creatures somewhere out there. They might be trying to get in touch with us by sending out radio signals. Scientists have searched for such signals, but so far they have not found any.

Did You Know That...

An astronaut can grow an inch or two taller on a long space mission. Because there is no gravity in space, the bones in an astronaut's spine can move slightly apart. But when the astronaut returns to earth, the gravity will soon shrink him back to his normal size.

Astronauts in space can communicate with earth by radio. Spacecraft and space instruments have to send messages to earth, but they can't do this by voice. They communicate by sending electronic signals. This is known as telemetry (tuh-LEM-uh-tree). The electronic signals are changed into pictures and words on earth. Scientists here can also use this method to send messages back to the spacecraft.

I HOPE TELEMETRY IS PICKING UP THE HUNGER MESSAGES FROM MY STOMACH.

In 1975 an American Apollo spacecraft docked and joined together with a Russian Soyuz that was orbiting the earth. The members of both crews shook hands and gave one another flags and medals. The crews worked together on experiments for two days. Both ships returned safely to earth at the end of the first successful joint mission by astronauts of two countries.

SHOO-BI DOO-BI DOO...

Scientists from different countries often work together on space projects. The countries of Western Europe have joined together and launched satellites into space. The countries of the world have to make special agreements about outer space. They have decided which radio channels to set aside for space communication. If they didn't, an astronaut might hear the latest popular song instead of hearing important instructions from ground control.

People cannot yet travel into deep space. So unmanned spacecraft have been sent on exploring missions. In 1976, the Viking 1 landed on Mars and sent the first Martian surface pictures to earth. The pictures showed reddish rocks and a pink sky. A mechanical arm of Viking 1 dug samples of Martian soil. The samples were placed in a mini laboratory that had been designed to test for life on Mars. Most scientists agree that these tests did not find life on Mars. But it is possible that some form of life might be found there someday.

View of Martian landscape transmitted by Viking 2

Voyagers 1 and 2 passed Jupiter in 1979. They sent back the first close-up pictures of the planet and its moons. The photos showed storms on Jupiter and a volcano erupting on Io, one of Jupiter's moons. The Voyagers also discovered a ring around Jupiter and the fourteenth moon of Jupiter. The ring and new moon are not visible from earth. It took a close-up view to give us this information.

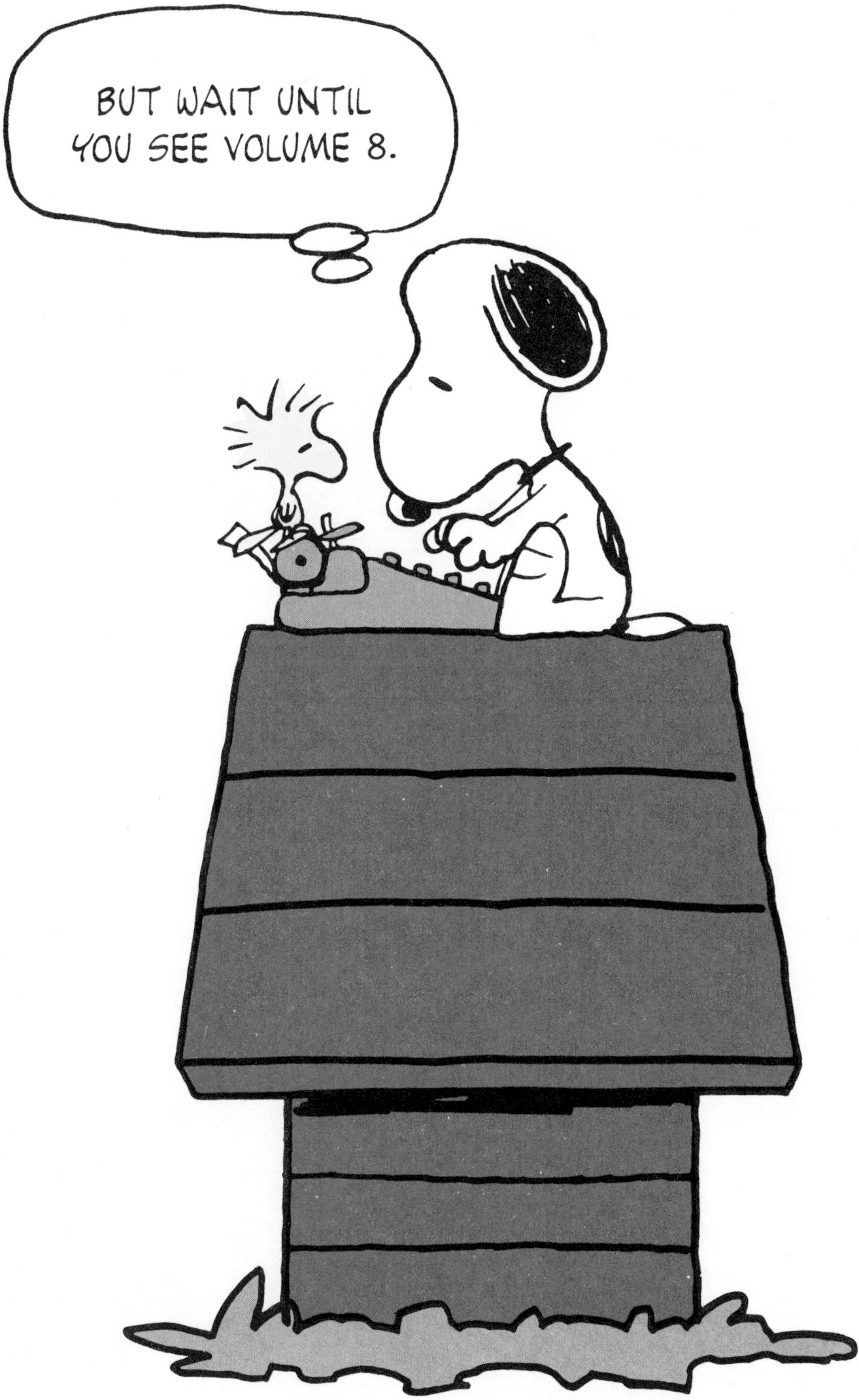
BUT WAIT UNTIL
YOU SEE VOLUME 8.